D0208558

Quiet Times

FOR MOTHERS

Julia Graham

© 2001 by Access Publishing

Available from
Church Resource Distributors
Phone (417) 831-7000

Contents

Introduction

Tuck this little book in your purse, your bedside table, your desk drawer at the office, by the coffeemaker in the kitchen — anyplace handy where you can use it quickly and regularly.

'Quiet time for mothers' almost sounds like a contradiction in terms. But quiet time with *God* can be like the miracle when Christ turned two fish and five loaves into enough food for five thousand men. Taking time with God somehow ends up leaving us with *more* time — a better *quality* of time — for everything else.

This book is compiled of selected quotes by women of faith, past and present. We trust these readings will be helpful — the beginning or continuation of many quiet times with God.

Trust His Ways

"Commit thy way unto the Lord; trust also in Him; and He shall bring it to pass" (Psalm 37:5).

"Having taken the step of faith by which you have put yourself wholly and absolutely into His hands, you must now expect Him to begin to work. His way of accomplishing that which you have entrusted to Him may be different from your way; but He knows and you must be satisfied.

I knew a lady who had entered into this life of faith ... with a wonderful flood of light and joy. She supposed this was a preparation for some great service ... Instead of this, almost at once, her husband lost all his money, and she was shut up to domestic duties, with no time or strength left for any Gospel work at all. She accepted the discipline, and yielded herself up as heartily to sweep, and dust, and bake, and sew, as she would have done to speak, or pray, or write for the Lord. And the result was that through this very training He made her into a vessel *'meet for the Master's use, and prepared unto every good work.'*

Another lady who had entered this life of faith under similar circumstances of wondrous blessing ... was shut up with two peevish invalid children to nurse and amuse all day long. Unlike the first one, this lady chafed and fretted, and finally rebelled, lost all her blessing, and went back into a state of sad coldness and misery. She had understood her part of trusting to begin with, but not understanding the Divine process of accomplishing that for which she had trusted, she took herself out of the hands of the Heavenly Potter, and the vessel was marred on the wheel. I believe many a vessel has been similarly marred by a want of understanding these things.

Hannah Whitall Smith (adapted)

"When trouble, restless fears, anxious fretfulness strive to overpower the soul, our safety is in saying, *'My God, I believe in Your perfect goodness and wisdom and mercy. What You are doing I cannot now understand, but I shall one day see it all plainly. Meanwhile I accept Your will, whatever it may be, unquestioning, without reserve.'*

There would be no restless disturbance, no sense of utter discomfort and discomposure in our souls, if we were quite free from any — it may be almost unconscious — opposition to God's will. But we do struggle against it, we do resist; and so long as that resistance endures we cannot be at peace. Peace, and even joy, are quite compatible with a great deal of pain — even mental pain — but never with a condition of antagonism or resistance."

Henrietta Louisa Sidney Lear

Thus will I live and walk
from day to day,
Contented, trustful, satisfied, and still.
What life so shielded, or what life
so free,
As that within the center of Thy will!

Jane Woodfall

Quiet Times

"Jesus got up very early ... and went to pray where there were no people" (Mark 1:35).

"You cannot expect to be victorious, if the day begins only in your own strength. Face the work of every day with the influence of a few thoughtful, quiet moments with your heart and God ... Meet Him alone. Meet Him regularly. Meet Him with His open Book of counsel before you, and face the regular (and irregular) duties of each day with the influence of His personality definitely controlling your every act."

Mrs. Charles C. Cowman

The Creator of the universe
wants to meet with you alone daily.
How can you say no
to such an opportunity?
Emilie Barnes

"How can a single weekly hour of church, helpful as it may be, counteract the many daily hours of distraction that surround us? If we had our contemplative hour at home we might be readier to give ourselves at church and find ourselves more completely renewed ... Quiet time alone ... prayer ... a centering time of thought or reading ..."

Anne Morrow Lindbergh

"I still believe that the planning, preparing, fixing, and organizing is important ... After all, I am trying to be faithful to do well the tasks He has set before me. I need to remember, though, that by far the most important thing I can do is to take the time to sit at Jesus' feet and really *listen*."

Mary Hampton

Think not again the wells of Life to fill,
By any conscious act of your own will;
Retire within the silence of your soul,
And let God's Spirit enter, and control.
The springs of feeling which you
thought were stilled,
Shall so be deepened, sweetened,
and refilled.
Anna J. Granniss

"Go into your private room when you pray, and pray to your Father who is in secret after you have shut your door. Your Father who sees what is done secretly, will reward you" (Matthew 6:6).

Ordinary Things

"The person who is faithful in little things is also faithful in big things" *(Luke 16:10).*

"It's the bits and pieces put together year after year that count. Sometimes we don't see meaning in the little things and we are not conscious of how it all works together to create a powerful image. The little things we do at home ... putting wildflowers in a vase ... an old photograph tucked into a frame, a lullaby each evening by the bedside ... are the putty that holds the mosaic together."

Ingrid Trobisch

"Ordinary work, which is what most of us do most of the time, is ordained by God every bit as much as is the extraordinary. All work done for God is spiritual work and therefore not merely a duty but a holy privilege."

Elisabeth Elliot

"Perfection in outward conduct consists not in extraordinary things; but in doing common things extraordinarily well. Neglect nothing ..."

Mere Angelique Arnauld

"It is easy to make great sacrifices when God does not ask them, but to give up our own will in each detail of life is something far harder. And this is what He does ask. To hold ourselves ever in readiness for His bidding — to count no token of it too slight — such is His call to each."

Hetty Bowman

"I felt very inadequate to do anything for the Lord, but one day I heard someone say that God does not expect us to be spectacular, He only asks us to be faithful. ... He needs us in all the little shattered corners where there are people hurting, needing encouragement. ... This is the beautiful part about ministering for Christ — we do not have to depend on our ability, strength or wisdom ... He will be there to enable us."

Sara Abram

So her life was full of sunshine,
for in toiling for the Lord
She had found the hidden sweetness
that in common things was stored.
Francesca Alexander

"There is no act too trifling to be made by God the first link in a chain of blessing."

Sarah W. Stephen

"Lord, give us a sense of satisfaction at the end of this day's work. Let us be able to look back on it, whatever its successes or failures ... with the knowledge that it was worth doing and that we did our best."

Marjorie Holmes

God's Ways

"So do not worry and say, 'What will we eat?' Or 'What will we drink?' Or 'What will we wear?' ... Your Father in heaven knows you need all these things. But seek His kingdom and His righteous ways first, and all these things will be given also to you" (Matthew 6:31-33).

Ten days before her wedding, Lillian Trasher received the call of God to serve in foreign missions. Despite the permanent parting from a man she loved, the 23-year-old answered the call, going to Egypt as a single woman with little means of support. She became a legend in that country, honored by the highest authorities for founding an orphanage which cared for thousands of unwanted children, who would otherwise have been left to die. She became a mother to the motherless, helping them grow up to lead useful and happy lives. She ran the orphanage on faith, subsisting day to day by God's provision. The following comes from her diary:

"November 12: 'All of our money gone again. I borrowed twenty dollars from Faheema, eight dollars and fifty cents from Farduse, and one dollar from Bobbie to pay the workmen. We haven't a cent.'

November 17: 'Busy all day making uniforms for the family. I hear from Cairo that all of Thomas Cook's Nile tourists are booked to come to the orphanage. I am trying to finish the uniforms so the children will look well.'

November 19: '... We are trying to have everything nice as we are expecting the tourists between four and five. I am tired. I do hope they will give me something for the children.

... The tourists all came, crowds and crowds of them ... the whole family of children went out to see the people ... I was proud of them. All who went up to the nursery were greatly touched as they saw the rows of tiny beds and wee babies in them, some with their bottles and others sitting on the carpet playing. While I was showing the tourists around a rather poor-looking old Egyptian walked down toward the main building.

I stopped and spoke to him, asking him to come in. He said, "No, not now." Some of the tourists handed Miss Ryott thirteen dollars for the orphanage.

After everyone left I saw the old man walking along and so again I asked him to come in. As he entered the drawing room he handed me a bill. It was fifty dollars.

I nearly laughed out loud. It was such a good lesson to me. I had been working all week to fix up the children and the place for the rich tourists and they gave me thirteen dollars, and a poor old Egyptian whom one scarcely notices, hands me a fifty-dollar bill! *God's ways are not our ways.*

Lillian Trasher

"From a weary laborer, worn with slavish and ineffectual toil, I had become as a little child receiving from God the free gift of eternal life and of daily sustenance — and prayer, from a weary spiritual exercise, had become the simple asking from the Heavenly Father of daily bread, and thanking Him."

Elizabeth Rundle Charles

Just As We Are

Just as I am, without one plea,
But that Thy blood was shed for me,
And that Thou bidd'st me come to Thee
… Just as I am, and waiting not
To rid my soul of one dark blot,
To Thee whose blood can cleanse each spot,
O Lamb of God, I come, I come.

Charlotte Eliott (1789-1871)

"Here lies the source of the rest He offers: If we come just as we are, He will welcome us. Spiritual fatigue, a burdened heart, the ugly mess we make of our lives … cause us to long for rest — any kind of rest from the inner and outer tensions against which we struggle … To expect such a troubled spirit to improve itself … to untangle its own problems, is … as impossible as to expect a man with two broken legs to sprint.

God offers the kind of inner rest that releases the energy we need to change our inadequacies to adequacies. … I have never known anyone who could do the job alone. Jesus must have seen it this way. Otherwise He would not have extended His inclusive invitation to *all* those who were in particular need of rest.

... Two things are necessary for us: we must see our need and we must come. The rest is up to God. And He can move into action in our behalf much more swiftly if we come — *just as we are*. Making no excuses, offering no explanations of how we got this way, expecting Him to act — not according to our idea of One who sits in judgment — rather, *as He is* ... a God of love.

... If we come *as we are*, expecting God to be there waiting *as He is*, we see at once that we are not the determining factor. God is."

Eugenia Price

"The one thing that more than any other keeps men from the Cross is the fact that the Cross stands for man's complete failure both to be and to do. 'Just as I am, without one plea,' is not the natural tendency of the human heart."

Anna J. Lindgren

Just as I am, though tossed about
With many a conflict, many a doubt,
Fightings and fears within, without ...
Just as I am, Thou wilt receive,
Wilt welcome, pardon, cleanse, relieve;
Because Thy promise I believe,
O Lamb of God, I come, I come.

Trouble Ahead?

"So do not worry about tomorrow"
(Matthew 6:34).

"An eminent Christian worker tells of his mother, who was a very anxious and troubled Christian. He would talk with her by the hour, trying to convince her of the sinfulness of fretting, but to no avail. (She was like the old lady who once said she had suffered so much, especially from the troubles that never came.)

But one morning the mother came down to breakfast wreathed in smiles ... and she told him that in the night she had a dream.

She was walking along a highway with a great crowd of people who seemed so tired and burdened. They were nearly all carrying little black bundles, and she noticed that there were numerous repulsive looking beings ... dropping these black bundles for the people to pick up and carry. Like the rest, she too had her needless load, and was weighed down with the devil's bundles. Looking up ... she saw a Man with a bright and loving face, passing through the crowd, and comforting the people.

At last He came near her, and she saw that it was her Saviour. She told him how tired she was, and He smiled sadly and said: 'My dear child, I did not give you these loads ... They are the devil's burdens and they are wearing out your life. Just drop them. Refuse to touch them ... and you will find the path easy and you will be as if borne on eagle's wings.'

He touched her hand ... Peace and joy thrilled her frame and flinging down her burden, she was about to throw herself at His feet in joyful thanksgiving, when suddenly she awoke and found that all her cares were gone. From that day to the close of her life she was the most cheerful and happy member of the household."

Mrs. Charles C. Cowman (adapted)

"A constant anticipation of evils which perhaps never will come, a foreboding which takes away life and energy from the present, will simply hinder and cloud the soul, and make it timid and sad.

If troubling thoughts as to the future will come ... the safest thing is to offer them continually as they arise to God ... asking for grace to concentrate our energies on the immediate duties surrounding us. Many have dreaded troubles which they thought must come; and while they went on always expecting them ... lo! they found that they had reached the journey's end ...

Even for others it is not wise to indulge in looking forward in fearfulness. Come what may to the dearest ones we have on earth, God and His upholding grace will be there, and He cares for them more than even we can do. An earnest commitment to His love will benefit them more than all our fretting."

Henrietta Louisa Sidney Lear (adapted)

"No one ever sank beneath the burden of the day! It's when tomorrow's burden is added to the burden of today that the weight is more than we can bear."

Author Unknown

Candle in the Heart

"And if anyone gives a cup of cold water to one of these little ones because he is my disciple, I tell you the truth, he will certainly not lose his reward" (Matthew 10:42 niv).

"The telephone rings.

... The caller is ... a bitter, malicious old woman who has divorced her husband, driven away her children, quarreled with her friends, and walked out of her church — and who is now eating her unrepentant soul out in loneliness and self-pity. (You're the only one for miles who still speaks to her, and you don't enjoy doing it.) Today she says ... she's absolutely desperate, and won't you come over and cheer her up? ... You think of all the times you've tried in vain to tell her of God and repentance and grace, only to be jeered at ...

You open your mouth to tell her, 'Sorry,

I can't come today, because I'm writing an article about Christ's commandment to love your neighbor —'

Oh, well. … You say, 'Be right over.'

… Well, you come back. You did cheer her up a little, after all. You're not any too cheerful yourself, thinking of your wasted working hours … and the old lady's poisoned darts … Nevertheless, deep inside you, there is a small bright glow. It's an unreasonable feeling … you've thrown away a day — a bit of your life — and got nothing in exchange for it. … Yet the small miraculous happiness persists.

… Take a good look at the brightness and recognize it for the love of God. Your love for Him and His for you … For one moment you forget the self and its desires and its rights; you gave a scrap of your life away, and in return you get this incredible candle in the heart for a moment."

Joy Davidman

"A kind word is never lost. It keeps going on and on, from one person to another, until at last it comes back to you again."

Anonymous

She now rarely lost
the sacred opportunity of
giving pleasure.
Sarah W. Stephen

"Life is a steep climb, and it does the heart good to have somebody 'call back' and cheerily beckon us on up the high hill. We are all climbers together, and we must help one another. This mountain climbing is serious business, but glorious. It takes strength and steady step to find the summits. The outlook widens with the altitude. If anyone among us has found anything worth while, we ought to 'call back.'"

(Selected)

Do you wish the world were happy?
Then remember day by day
Just to scatter seeds of kindness
As you pass along the way.
Ella Wheeler Wilcox

Our Part, God's Part

"'I will put my laws in their hearts, and I will write them in their minds,' says the Lord" (Hebrews 10:16).

"(In this higher life) there is a certain work to be accomplished ... Besetting sins are to be conquered; evil habits are to be overcome; wrong dispositions and feelings are to be rooted out, and holy tempers and emotions are to be begotten. A positive transformation is to take place.

... Now somebody must do this. Either we must do it for ourselves or another must do it for us. Most of us have tried ... and have grievously failed. Then we discover the Lord Jesus Christ has come on purpose to do it and that He will do it for all who put themselves wholly into His hands and trust Him without reserve.

When we say, therefore, that ... man's part is to trust, and God's part is to do the thing entrusted to Him, we do not surely present any very difficult or puzzling problem.

... The one who is speaking on man's part in the matter cannot speak of anything but surrender and trust, because this is positively all the man can do.

... (But) when we trust, the Lord works, and a great deal is done, not by us, but by Him. Actual results are reached by our trusting, because our Lord undertakes the thing entrusted to Him, and accomplishes it."

Hannah Whitall Smith (adapted)

"(The higher life) is to be ... ingrafted into the vine, to have no impediment remaining to hinder the flow of the sap; and while the soul thus abides by faith it brings forth much fruit ..."

Mary Fletcher

God has given us a will
to choose His will.

Henrietta C. Mears

Maybe Tomorrow

"So then faith cometh by hearing, and hearing by the word of God" (Romans 10:17).

"I went a long way in life before I really learned to love God's Word. I intended to read it every day, but I was busy. I'd get out of bed and have to get the kids dressed for school, then as a pastor's wife I had to get the dishes done — I couldn't let anyone catch me with dirty dishes in the sink! And of course, I had to get the beds made and the house presentable. Then the phone began to ring and that day was in motion and I was in motion.

Before I knew it, night-time had come, and I'd fall into bed exhausted. I'd pick up the Word, feeling under conviction because I hadn't read it. I'd read the same verse over six times and still not remember what I read. Finally I'd close it up and say, 'Tomorrow I'll read it.' The next day the same thing would happen.

Some years ago I was sitting in a camp meeting where my husband was one of the speakers. Another speaker was preaching on the power of the Word. The Holy Spirit shone His spotlight into my heart. He said, 'Do you know why you are so disappointed with yourself as a Christian and a wife and a mother? It's because you're anemic! You're not feeding on My Word.'

Sitting on that rough bench, I lifted up my heart and made a vow and commitment, 'God, I will partake of your Word every day.' That was a hard one for me to make, because it is so hard for me to get up in the morning. But He was there to help me, and I've done it. He has changed my life by it, and through that the atmosphere in our home.

One lady said she achieved serenity in her home when she started making sure of having seven minutes with God every morning. Seven minutes may not seem much, but it's a whole lot better than nothing. And you can be amazed what seven minutes with God ... reading one or two Scriptures and letting Him take over in your heart for a few minutes ... can do to prepare you to set the atmosphere in your life and home.

Napoleon once said, *'The Bible is not just a mere book, it is a living force with the power to conquer all that opposes it.'* And that includes all of the forces that would oppose you in your daily life.

I used to have to make myself read the Bible, but now I love it. When I read it, the Holy Spirit takes it and plants it deep into the soil of my heart. As I go through the day, I find that He brings His Word to my remembrance, applied as a soft, gentle guidance and caution and strength, just when I need it."

Sara Abram

"For as long as I can remember the Word of God has been the place for me to go for answers and direction — my fundamental guide in making decisions."

Gloria Gaither

"The only way I can increase my faith, according to the Bible, is to read it, and meditate on it. Just read it, and read it, and read it, until it works into my system ..."

Donna Fargo

Who Has Our Moments?

"What is man ... that You should set Your mind upon him ... every morning ... every moment?" (Job 7:17,18)

Born in 1836, Frances Ridley Havergal was a talented musician and poet who devoted her talents to God. Despite ill-health, she became a well-known writer. The words of the famous hymn, 'Take My Life, and Let It Be' came to her in the night, after leading ten people to Christ. Just before her death, she finished a book with chapter headings taken from the words of this hymn.

Take my moments and my days;
Let them flow in ceaseless praise.

"We consider some of the practical details of the life which we desire to have 'kept' for Jesus in the hymn ... with the one word *'take'* changed to *'keep.'* ... The first point that naturally comes up is almost synonymous with life — our time.

... When a New Year comes round, we commit it with special earnestness to the Lord. But as we do so, are we not conscious of a feeling that even a year is too much for us to deal with?

... Then as the Monday mornings come round, we thankfully commit the opening week to Him ... But not even the six or seven days are close enough to our hand; even tomorrow exceeds our tiny grasp ... So we find the need of considering our lives as a matter of day by day ... But if we commit the days to our Lord, why not the hours, and why not the moments?

... Do you ask, 'But what use can He make of mere moments?' Look back ... how often a great work grew out of a mere moment in the life of one of God's servants ... It is not so often a whole sermon as a single short sentence that wings God's arrow to a heart. It is seldom a whole conversation ... but some sudden turn of thought which comes with the electric touch of God's power. Sometimes only a look (and what is more momentary?) has been used by Him ... Oh, how much we have missed by not placing our moments at His disposal!

... We do not see this as long as the moments are kept in our own hands. We are like little children closing our fingers over diamonds. How can they reflect the rays of light while they are shut up tight in the dirty little hands? ... Let Him always keep them for us, and then we shall always see His light and love reflected in them. And then surely they shall be filled with praise. Not that we are to be always singing hymns ... but praise will be the color, the atmosphere in which they will flow.

... Is it a little too much for them all to flow in ceaseless praise? Well, where will you stop? What proportions of your moments do you think enough for Jesus?

... He made you ... He chose you ... He loves you every moment ... watches you unslumberingly, cares for you unceasingly ... He died for you! ... Shall you or I remember all this love and hesitate to give all our moments up to Him?"

Frances Ridley Havergal (adapted)

Lord, my time is in Thine hand,
Weak and helpless as I am,
Surely Thou canst make me stand.
Hymn

Sweetbriar Roses

"'For I know the thoughts that I think toward you,' says the Lord, 'thoughts of peace, and not of evil, to give you hope and a future'" (Jeremiah 29:11).

Writings for people who suffer are most comforting when they come from those who have experienced suffering. Amy Carmichael qualified for this, writing from twenty years of illness and pain experienced in the midst of the great mission work she founded in India.

"I believe that He can give it to us to find something truly lovable in that which (while He allows it to continue) is His will for us. Disappointments, for example ...

After the foot began to mend, other troubles came, one after the other, pulling me up just when it seemed as though I might soon be able to walk.

... I had set my heart on being at the Welcome Service. ... For a month or so before that date it had seemed that this would be. Then the hope gradually faded. I was still in bed ... not even in a chair. That morning, while the chiming bells of welcome were being rung ... I ached to be there ... and then, each word as clear as though it slid down the clear chiming bells, this little song sang within me:

Thou has not *that*, My child,
but Thou hast Me,
And am I not alone enough for thee?
... I know it all;
but from thy brier shall blow
A rose for others. ...
Come, then, say to Me,
'My Lord, My Love,
I am content with Thee.'

'*From thy brier shall blow a rose for others.*' ... Called to mind by these words, I saw a little, low, very prickly bush in an old-fashioned English garden; it was covered with inconspicuous pink roses. But the wonder of the bush was its all-pervading fragrance, for it was a sweetbrier.

... I think that when He comes so near to us, and so gently helps our human weakness ... we find a secret sweetness in our brier. But it is not of us. It is Love that lifts us up ... Love that is the sweetness.

Is the one who reads this in a great weariness, or the exhaustion that follows a sore hurt, or in the terrible grasp of pain? He who loves us as no one else can love, who understands to the uttermost, is not far away. He wants us to say, He can give it to us to say, 'My Lord, my Love, I am content with Thee.'"

Amy Carmichael (adapted)

"It must be that when the Lord took from me one faculty, He gave me another ... I think of the beautiful Italian proverb: 'When God shuts a door, He opens a window.'"

Helen Keller

"George Matheson, the blind preacher of Scotland, said, 'My God, I have never thanked Thee for my thorn. I have thanked Thee a thousand times for my roses, but not once for my thorn. ... Teach me the value of my thorn ... Show me that I have climbed to Thee by the path of pain. Show me that my tears have made my rainbows.'"

Mrs. Charles C. Cowman

The Comforter

"I will pray the Father, and He shall give you another Comforter, that He may be with you for ever ... the Comforter, even the Holy Spirit, whom the Father will send in My name, He shall teach you all things" (John 14:16,26 asv).

"Whatever God asks you to do, if you are open and yielded to His Holy Spirit, He will be enough. He will qualify you to do the work He gives you, enabling you in life's pressure and stress. Christ told His disciples, *'I won't leave you comfortless. My Father will send the Comforter.'*

When I was a little girl, we lived on a farm in Minnesota with my grandmother. There was no central heating. We had a pot-bellied stove downstairs, and upstairs nothing but the chimney going through the bedroom. When the Minnesota winter nights got down to 30-below, we'd dress around the stove downstairs, put on our pajamas, and leave our socks on. Then I would tear up those stairs as fast as I could and dive into that bed. Do you know how cold blankets can get? But there was one redeeming factor. My grandmother had a feather-filled comforter. When I got under that comforter, it was light and put no weight on me, but it provided the cozy comfort of warmth. That's the way it is with the Comforter God sent us. He doesn't put a load on us. He doesn't put weight on us, but He is there, just warming us in His love and His comfort and His guidance."

Sara Abram

I cannot, but God can;
Oh, balm for all my care!
The burden that I drop
His hand will lift and bear
... This is my strength: to know
I cannot, but God can.

Author Unknown

"As one may have all the air that he is able to breathe, so may one have all the aid of the Holy Spirit which he is capable of receiving. Man can never accept as gladly and freely as God offers, but in just the proportion to which he can ... to that degree God fills his life with a glory not of earth."

Lilian Whiting (adapted)

There Isn't Time

"Forgive a person when you pray, if you have anything against him, so your Father who is in heaven will also forgive you for your sins" (Mark 11:25).

"Love ... can only be the gift of God. Yet He cannot give us that gift so long as bitterness and resentment have slammed shut the door of the heart and unforgiveness stands sentinel at the door lest love open and enter. Forgiveness is the precondition of love.

The 'how' of forgiveness is through knowing how to use our will — the rudder of our life. We are responsible for the set of this rudder; once we have willed a course of action, God will be responsible for the feelings if we will hand them over to Him. Otherwise, nothing we can do would change these feelings.

... David du Plessis' (said), *'Forgiveness means, "The other person may be as wrong as wrong can be, but I'll not be the judge."'*

I saw that forgiveness is simply the decision of our wills to release a particular person, followed by verbalizing that to God. It can be a simple prayer like, *'Lord, I release _____ from my judgment. Forgive me that I may have ... hampered your work by judging. Now I step out of the way so that Heaven can go into action for _____.'* Obviously, there is nothing impossible about praying like that.

Catherine Marshall

If I take offense easily, if I am content to
continue in a cool unfriendliness,
though friendship be possible, then I
know nothing of Calvary love.
Amy Carmichael

"It will be appropriate ... to ask ourselves, Is there any false friend or subtle enemy whom we must learn to tolerate, to bear with, to pity and forgive? Can we in silent love wash their feet as our Master washed the feet of Judas?

And, if we have no real enemies, are there any bound to us in the relations of life whose habits and ways are annoying and distasteful to us?

Can we bear with them in love ... and

change censoriousness of others into prayer for ourselves?"

Harriet Beecher Stowe (adapted)

"Misunderstandings will come and perhaps there will be a measure of right and wrong on both sides. The little momentary break must not be allowed to widen. ... Three golden phrases will do wonders in such unhappy hours. *'I was wrong'* — *'I am sorry'* — *'Please forgive me.'* It is hard sometimes to acknowledge any mistake; but the healing of even the tiniest breach is well worth the effort made. The sooner these words are sincerely spoken the easier they are to say."

Alice Reynolds Flower

If hurt today by what men say,
If wounded by a friend,
Oh, let tonight set all things right,
Let trouble have an end.
... Life isn't long, just time for song,
And love, and things sublime.
Be not concerned with thoughts that burned,
Good friends, there isn't time.

Author unknown

The Lord My Shepherd

"Jesus ... was moved with compassion toward them, because they were as sheep not having a shepherd" (Mark 6:34).

"Perhaps no aspect in which the Lord reveals himself to us is fuller of genuine comfort than in the Twenty-third Psalm. ... *'The Lord is my shepherd, I shall not want.'* Who is it that is your shepherd? ... The Almighty Creator ... He who holds the universe in His hand as though it were a very little thing, He is your Shepherd, and has charged himself with the care and keeping of you, as a shepherd is charged with the care and keeping of his sheep.

I had a vivid experience of this at one time in my Christian life ... There came a critical moment when I was sadly in need of comfort ... I could not lay hand on my Bible, and I cast about in my mind for some Scripture that would help me. There flashed into my mind the words, *'The Lord is my shepherd, I shall not want.'* 'Such a common text as that,' I said to myself, 'is not likely to do me any good.' I tried hard to think of a more *recherche* one, but none would come ... finally I said, 'Well, I must try to get what little good I can out of this one,' and I began to repeat to myself over and over, *'The Lord is my shepherd, I shall not want.'* Suddenly the words were divinely illuminated, and there poured out upon me such floods of comfort that I felt as if I could never have a trouble again.

The moment I could get hold of a Bible, I (searched) with eagerness to see whether it could possibly be true that such untold treasures of comfort were really mine, and whether I might dare let out my heart into the full enjoyment of them ... I built up a pyramid of declarations and promises concerning the Lord being our Shepherd, that, once built, presented an indestructible front to all the winds and storms of doubt or trial that could assail it. And I became convinced, beyond a shadow of doubt, that the Lord really was my Shepherd, and that in giving himself this name He assumed the duties belonging to the name, and really would be what He declares himself ... a *'good shepherd who giveth His life for His sheep.'*

... Perhaps you will say, 'But I am so weak and foolish and ignorant, that I am not worthy of His care.' But do you not know that sheep are always weak, and helpless, and silly; and that is the very reason they are compelled to have a shepherd ... Their welfare and safety do not depend upon their own strength, but wholly upon the care of their shepherd.

... The part of the sheep is very simple ... to trust and to follow. The Shepherd does all the rest. He leads ... He chooses paths where they can walk in safety. ... The sheep have none of the planning to do, none of the decisions to make ... nothing to do but trust themselves entirely to the care of the good Shepherd and follow Him.

... There is nothing complicated about it. It is simply to believe it, and act as if it were true. ... Say, *'This is my psalm, and I am going to believe that the Lord really is my Shepherd and that He will care for me ... I will not doubt nor question it again.'* And then just abandon yourself to His care."

Hannah Whitall Smith (adapted)

It's Impossible

"It is impossible for people, but it is not impossible for God, because all things are possible with God" (Mark 10:27).

"I went to America some years ago with the captain of a steamer, who was a very devoted Christian. When off the coast of Newfoundland he said to me, 'The last time I crossed here ... something happened which revolutionized the whole of my Christian life. We had George Mueller on board. I had been on the bridge twenty-four hours and never left it.

George Mueller came to me and said, "Captain, I have come to tell you that I must be in Quebec Saturday afternoon."

"It is impossible," I said.

"Very well, if your ship cannot take me, God will find some other way. I have never broken an engagement for fifty-seven years. Let us go down into the chart-room and pray."

I looked at that man of God, and

thought to myself, What lunatic asylum can that man have come from? I never heard of such a thing as this. "Mr. Mueller,' I said, 'do you know how dense this fog is?"

"No," he replied, "my eye is not on the density of the fog, but on the living God, who controls every circumstance of my life."

He knelt down and prayed one of the most simple prayers, and when he finished I was going to pray, but he put his hand on my shoulder, and told me not to pray. "First, you do not believe He will answer; and second, I believe He has, and there is no need whatever for you to pray about it."

I looked at him, and he said, "Captain, I have known my Lord for fifty-seven years, and there has never been a single day that I have failed to get audience with the King. Get up, Captain, and open the door, and you will find the fog gone."

I got up, and the fog was indeed gone. On Saturday afternoon, George Mueller was in Quebec for his engagement.'"

(Selected) Mrs. Charles C. Cowman

"He is able to do much more than we can ever ask for or think of, by His power that works in us" (Ephesians 3:20).

"Some of us believe that God is all mighty, and may do all — and that He is all wisdom, and can do all — but that He is all love, and *will* do all, there we fail."

Mother Juliana

Bees and Buzzards

"Love is patient and kind ... It does not become angry easily, and it does not remember wrong things that are done ... It believes all things, hopes for all things and endures all things" (1 Corinthians 13:4,5,7).

"Bees and buzzards are very different ... buzzards circle above, looking for animals that are hurt or dead. Then they swoop down to tear on it. Honeybees are the exact opposite. They look only for the good sweet nectar, as they fly from flower to flower. Both buzzards and bees find what they're looking for — just as a wife can usually find what she's looking for in her husband. She'll see what she wants to see: the good — or the bad.

If we focus on our husbands' faults and mistakes, we'll find them. And the more fault we find, the less we'll respect them. When a husband feels that his wife doesn't respect him ... guess who's the last person he wants to be with?

But if we try to look for the good qualities in our husbands and focus on those, we can grow to respect and admire them. When they feel this respect from us, because we stop cutting them down and criticizing them, our marriages will be much happier. A wise person said:

'To your husband's qualities and good
points, be very kind,
To his faults and mistakes,
a little blind.'

A husband needs to know that home is a safe place where he won't be criticized and put down the minute he walks in the door. If we could just guard and control our words and attitudes, think how peaceful our homes could be.

There was a young married couple who really struggled to make enough money to live on. One day the husband took the little they had and bought a small service station. His wife didn't think this was a good investment — she knew he didn't have the time or knowledge to run the service station. The station soon went broke and they lost everything. The husband came home expecting his wife to be angry and to remind him that she'd told him not to do it. Instead she sat down with him and said, 'I've been doing some figuring. You don't smoke or drink alcohol, but if you had, we would have lost just as much money as we did with the service station. So don't worry, let's just forget it.'

She could so easily have destroyed her husband's self-confidence that day. Instead she let him know she still believed in him. He went on to become a wonderful minister, known nation-wide.

There's a big difference between us and buzzards and bees. God made us so we can *choose* what we want to think, say and do. But learning self-control and acceptance is much easier said than done. It's only with Christ's kind of love that we can do it! If we ask Him to help us, He'll fill our hearts with His love so we can give our husbands the respect and confidence they need from us."

Tia Stanley

"Study your husband as you would a rare plant. Minimize his faults and enlarge upon his virtues. After you have talked upon his good qualities for some time, you will be surprised to find you believe what you say."

Lilla Gertrude English, from *'Love Lights for Maid, Wife and Mother'* (1912)

A Key to Victory

"I will bless the Lord at all times. His praise shall continually be in my mouth" (Psalm 34:1).

"Whether it's a financial crunch, a sudden illness, or a personal defeat, if you fix your heart on praise to God, then you have offered a sacrifice.

... It's like saying, 'I have prayed about this burden, and now, Lord, I will quietly wait on You even before I see the answer. I expect it. And this is my sacrifice of praise to You — I believe and trust.'

... Most of the verses written about praise in God's Word were voiced by people faced with crushing heartaches, injustice, treachery, slander, and scores of other difficult situations. They knew that the sacrifice of praise was a key to victory on their spiritual journey."

Joni Eareckson Tada

"Set aside a regular devotional time for thanksgiving. At first it will not be easy. Requests fall from human lips with greater ease than praise."

Anne Allan

"If our hearts were tuned to praise, we should see causes unnumbered, which we had never seen before, for thanking God. Thanksgiving is spoken of as a *'sacrifice well pleasing unto God.'* It is a far higher offering than prayer. When we pray we ask for things we want, or we tell our sorrows. We pray in order to bring down blessings upon ourselves ... *Praise* flows out of love, and then the love goes back to our hearts, and warms them anew.

... Begin with thanking Him for some little thing, and then go on, day by day, adding to your subjects of praise ... You will find their numbers grow wonderfully, and in the same proportion, will your subjects of murmuring and complaining diminish, until you see in everything some cause for thanksgiving.

If you cannot begin with anything positive, begin with something negative. ... There is some trial that has *not* been appointed you, and you may thank God for its being withheld from you. It is certain that the more you try to praise, the more you will see how your path and your lying down are beset with mercies and that the God of love is ever watching to do you good."

Priscilla Maurice (adapted)

Does your Heavenly Father give you
many blessings here below?
Then on bended knee before Him,
frankly, gladly, tell Him so!

Geraldine Searfoss

Walk Cheerfully

"For as he thinketh within himself, so is he ... " Proverbs 23:7.

"A vexation arises, and our expressions of impatience hinder others from taking it patiently. Disappointment, ailment, or even weather depresses us — and our look or tone of depression hinders others from maintaining a cheerful and thankful spirit ... Wrong feeling is even more infectious than wrongdoing, especially the various phases of ill temper — gloominess, touchiness, discontentedness, irritability. Do we not know how *catching* these are?"

Frances Ridley Havergal

Walk cheerfully
and freely in God's service.
St. Teresa

"All encounters in life, every personality, every institution, every relationship, is a mixture of the good and the bad. When we habitually focus on the bad, we are training ourselves in negativism. ... There is a secret cost in such an outlook to one's spiritual and mental health. In my case, I woke up twenty years into adulthood to find myself deeply schooled in serious negativism. That, in turn, can bathe all of life in emotional gloom. When the habit continues ... the dark glasses of criticalness can lead to long periods of melancholy and even to serious depression."

Catherine Marshall

"I find that it is not the circumstances in which we are placed, but the spirit in which we meet them, that constitutes our comfort — and this comfort may be undisturbed, if we seek for and cherish a feeling of quiet submission, whatever may come to us."

Elizabeth T. King (adapted)

To *be* happy
is properly the beginning of all schemes
for *making* happy.
Sarah W. Stephen

"We are in danger of forgetting that God is not only a comfort but a joy. He is the source of all pleasures; He is fun and light and laughter, and we are meant to enjoy Him ... *'Thou shalt not enjoy life'* was never Christ's teaching ... To be Christian is to be reborn, and free, and unafraid and immortally young."

Joy Davidman

The Richest Years

"The righteous ... will still bear fruit in old age, they will stay fresh and green, proclaiming, 'The Lord ... is my Rock.'"
(Psalm 92:12,14,15 niv)

"The fiftieth milestone in my calendar of years had been reached when ... Providence changed the entire course of my life. I was confronted with the question, 'After fifty years, what?'

I then read the following statement: *'The greatest years of a woman's life come after fifty. Until that time she is accumulating new experiences. At fifty she has traveled every road. Now should come the harvest years. If a woman will keep intellectually alive, spiritually aglow and with heart aflame, with a passion for living service, she will see her greatest years from fifty to seventy-five.'*

Today in my eighty-second year I would bear witness to the fact that the years since that memorable experience — the crisis year — have been the richest, and the fullest and the sweetest of any of my long lifetime."

Mrs. Charles C. Cowman

For is it not true that
middle age
can be looked upon as a period
of second flowering,
second growth?
Anne Morrow Lindbergh

"People who talk of going down the hill in late middle life are not happy. Happy, contented people keep on climbing till they reach eternity, life's highest peak."

Ann Allan

"A man who had preserved his youth, not only in appearance, but in heart, long after he had reached the limit of three score and ten, gave as his reason, *'I have always looked forward to each new day eagerly. I know there will be something in it for me to learn, to enjoy. There will be unexpected blessings and surprises. There will be trials — perhaps sorrow — but I have learned to look upon them all as lessons which must be learned in this school of life ... I welcome them as friends. Every day there come chances for putting happiness into the lives of others, opportunities large and small for serving my Master ... I greet every new day with joy, for I know ... that it will hold for me something good."*

Anne Guilbert Mahon

"The only way to remain young is to grow old gracefully. Each age has something beautiful in it. Don't fight the fact that you are getting old — use it."

Author Unknown

"At eighty years of age, the great poet, Edwin Markham, wrote 'The Look Ahead,' which ends:

I laugh and lift hands to
the years ahead:
'Come on, I am ready for you.'

Limitations

"I begged the Lord three times to take this problem away from me, and He said to me, 'My grace is enough for you, because My power is made perfect in weakness.' I will have pride in my weaknesses and have joy because of them, so Christ's power can be in me" (2 Corinthians 12:8-9).

"For each one of us — whether on a bed of pain, in the feebleness and uncertainty of purpose which can come with ill-health or overstrained nerves, or whatever else may be our immediate condition — nothing is more urgent than for us to ask, 'What would You have me to do?'

For whatever our state, however helpless and incapable, however little service to God or to our neighbor seems to be within our power, there is no doubt at all as to His willing us to do something.

Not necessarily any great thing — it may be only some little message of sympathy and comfort to one even more lonely than we are — it may be a kindly word or glance to one whose own fault has cut him off from general kindness and pity — it may be even just to stand and wait in humble patience till He makes His will plain, refusing to murmur or fret while we wait — but in some shape or other, be certain that your Master and Lord hears and will answer your question, 'What would You have me to do?'"

H. L. Sidney Lear (adapted)

"Know who you are and accept yourself. Don't covet someone else's abilities, but recognize your own assets and use them. Also accept your limitations. God doesn't ask you to account for what you don't have. Isn't that a relief? The Lord puts less pressure on us than anyone in the world, because He know us as we really are. He knows our motives. He also knows our physical limitations and strength. This is a hard lesson for me to learn ... but I keep trusting the Lord to help me. I see so many needs, yet I am limited in strength and I can get very, very discouraged. But that doesn't accomplish anything.

Remember that the Lord knows and understands your physical limitations — better than you, than anyone. So *you* must accept them and then choose wisely what you are going to do with the physical strength that you do have."

Sara Abram

Is it the Lord that shuts me in?
Then I can bear to wait!
No place so dark, no place so poor,
So strong and fast no prisoning door ...
But out of it goes fair and broad
An unseen pathway, straight to God.
Susan Coolidge

"In my attempts to promote the comfort of my family, the quiet of my spirit has been disturbed. Some of this is doubtless owing to physical weakness ... This is of great importance, to watch carefully — now I am so weak — not to overfatigue myself, because then I cannot contribute to the pleasure of others. And a placid face and a gentle tone will make my family more happy than anything else I can do for them."

Elizabeth T. King

This is the Way

"That the Lord ... may tell us the way in which we should walk and the thing that we should do" (Jeremiah 42:3 nasb).

"If you really do purpose to obey the Lord in every respect, and your soul only needs to know the will of God in order to consent to it, then you surely cannot doubt His willingness to make His will known, and to guide you in the right paths. There are many very clear promises in reference to this.

... We come now to the question as to how God's guidance is to come to us, and how we shall be able to know His voice.

There are four ways in which He reveals His will to us — through the Scriptures, through providential circumstances, through the convictions of our own higher judgment, and through the inward impressions of the Holy Spirit on our minds.

Where these four harmonize, it is safe

to say that God speaks. ... Above all else, trust Him. ... He has promised to guide. You have asked Him to do it. And now you must believe that He does ... God cannot guide those who never trust Him enough to believe He is doing it."

Hannah Whitall Smith

Reach up as far as you can
and God will reach down
all the rest of the way.

Author Unknown

"The Shepherd said ... 'When you continue your journey there may be much mist and cloud. Perhaps it may even seem as though everything you have seen here of the High Places was just a dream, or the work of your own imagination. But you have seen reality, and the mist which seems to swallow it up is the illusion.

'Believe steadfastly in what you have seen. Even if the way up ... appears to be obscured and you are led to doubt whether you are following the right path, remember the promise. *"Thine ears shall hear a word behind thee, saying, 'This is the way, walk ye in it, when ye turn to the right hand and when ye turn to the left.'"*

Always go forward along the path of obedience as far as you know it until I intervene ...

'Remember ... what you have seen before the mist blotted it out. Never doubt that the High Places are there ... and be quite sure that whatever happens I mean to bring you up there exactly as I have promised.'"

Hannah Hurnard

No matter how steep your mountain,
The Lord will climb it with you.
Edna Louise Gilbert

Waiting

*"I wait for You, O Lord; You will answer"
(Psalm 38:15 niv).*

"A soul, who made rapid progress in her
understanding of the Lord, was once asked
the secret of her easy advancement.

She replied tersely, *'Mind the checks.'*

And the reason that many of us do not
know and better understand Him is, we do
not give heed to His gentle checks ... His is
a still, small voice. A still voice can hardly
be heard. It must be felt. A steady, gentle
pressure upon the heart and mind ... a
small voice, quietly spoken in your heart,
but if heeded growing noiselessly clearer to
your inner ear.

... In conversation, when about to utter
some word, give heed to that gentle voice,
mind the check and refrain from speech.
When about to pursue some course that
seems all clear and right and there comes
quietly to your spirit a suggestion that has
in it the force almost of a conviction, give

heed, even if changed plans seem folly from the standpoint of human wisdom. Learn also to wait on God for the unfolding of His will. Let God form your plans ... and then let Him execute them.

Simply listen, obey and trust God ... He will in the end make *'all things work together.'*

... So if you would know His voice, never consider results or possible effects. Obey even when He asks you to move in the dark. ... And there will spring up rapidly in your heart an acquaintanceship and a fellowship with God which will hold you and Him together, even in severest testings."

Way of Faith (adapted)

"A person once said to a friend, 'I am quite at a loss to know which way to turn.' 'Then don't turn at all,' was the friend's wise reply."

Unknown

Wait, patiently wait,
God never is late.
Mercy A. Gladwin

After the Darkness

"For, lo, the winter is past; the rain is over and gone; the flowers appear on the earth" (Song of Solomon 2:11,12).

"When the ground in London was cleared of the old buildings ... it lay for a year exposed to the light and air. A strange sight drew naturalists to the ruins. In some cases the soil had not felt the touch of spring since the day when the Romans sailed up the Thames.

... When the sunlight poured its life upon this uncovered soil, a host of flowers sprang up. Some were unknown in England. They were plants the Romans had brought with them. Hidden away in the darkness ... under the mass of bricks and mortar, they seemed to have died, but under the new conditions, obeying the law of life, they escaped from death and blossomed into a new beauty.

So may it be with every life, however crushed and bruised by sorrow, however blighted by sin. It needs only to be laid open to the breath of God's Spirit, the sunshine of His love, and the healing atmosphere of His grace in Christ Jesus, and a new life with new possibilities and new beauties, will arise, however desolate at present the scene may appear."

Mrs. Charles C. Cowman

"The power of the Resurrection ... vanquishes every other power in heaven or earth. The battle was the bitterest ever fought, but death was the loser, Jesus the Victor ... Sin and death need not hold us either ... Hatred, self-pity, bitterness, resentment — these are tombs. By the power that raised Jesus Christ from that sealed and guarded tomb we may be delivered from whatever seals us off from life. Jesus came to give us life, nothing less than ... 'abundant' life."

Elisabeth Elliot

"I believe that God is in me as the sun is in the colour and fragrance of a flower — the Light in my darkness, the Voice in my silence."

Helen Keller

Two-Way

"Call to Me, and I will answer you, and I will tell you great and mightly things, which you do not know" (Jeremiah 33:3 nasb).

"Do you sometimes wonder why you didn't get what you prayed for? Well, do you sit back after you pray and wait for God to bring you what you want, like a waiter at a restaurant? Someone said: 'We are a part of the answer to every prayer that we pray.' It could be that while we're waiting for God to do something, He's waiting for us to do our part.

You see, prayer is a two-way conversation. Prayer isn't our getting God to do what we want — it's more God trying to tell us what He wants, so we can learn how to live a successful, satisfying life. … Imagine if God always gave us everything we asked for. Then we would just give Him our orders, forget Him, and go on living our own way. But God created each of us to enjoy a daily, personal relationship with Him. So maybe He's not giving us exactly what we're asking for, in order to get our attention, so we'll start getting closer to Him, to listen and learn His way of living. Because prayer doesn't only change things, prayer changes us.

Sometimes God wants us to wait, even when we ask Him for good things, because He knows our real motives are wrong. Perhaps we're asking God to change someone else instead of changing *us*. The problem or difficult person may not go away because God wants us to change our heart and attitude toward that person or problem.

Through prayer we become closer to our Maker and learn to trust Him. You see, He's doing what is best in the long run, not only for us, but for everyone else involved. He's the only One who can see the big picture, or jigsaw puzzle, of life. He knows how everything fits together, now and in years to come.

We usually enjoy people we can be real with, because pretending to be someone you're not is tiring! We want our friends to be natural and real with us. And that's how God wants us to talk to Him! When Christ taught His followers how to pray, He used the everyday street language of His culture.

God wants us to be ourselves with Him — to tell Him how we feel and think, just as we would with our closest friends. God wants to have a good, heart-to-heart talk with you … every day!"

Tia Stanley

"Perhaps prayer often needs to be followed by a little pause, that we may have time to open our hearts to that for which we have prayed. We often rush from prayer to prayer without waiting for the word within, which says, *'I have heard you, My child.'*"

Amy Carmichael

"It is an ongoing process, not just an occasional religious-sounding speech … Prayer is meant to be a part of our lives, like breathing and thinking and talking."

Gloria Gaither

"God is not found in multiplicity, but in simplicity of thoughts and words. If one word suffices for your prayer, keep to that word, and to whatever short sentence will unite your heart with God."

Margaret Mary Hallaran

Think About It

"Think about things that are true, right, pure, lovely, and excellent ... things that bring honor, things that are respected, and things that are good enough to receive praise" (Philippians 4:8).

"The things we think on are the things that feed our souls. If we think on pure and lovely things we shall grow pure and lovely like them, and the opposite is equally true. Very few people realize this, and consequently they are careless in regard to their thoughts. They guard their words and actions with care, but their thoughts, which after all are the very spring and root of everything in character and life, they neglect entirely. So long as it is not put into spoken words, it seems of no consequence at all as to what goes on within the mind. No one hears or knows, and therefore they imagine that the vagrant thoughts that come and go do no harm.

Such persons are very careless as to the

food offered to their thoughts and accept without discrimination anything that comes ... The laws of hygiene are as absolute in the realm of spirit as in the realm of the physical ... These laws work on inexorably, whether we know it or not; and unconsciously we may be degrading our soul life by the thoughts we are indulging, the books we are reading, or the company we are keeping.

... Neither will little doses of suitable food now and then do. One hour of a Christ-like way of looking at things will not make much headway in the matter of the soul's health against ten hours of unchristian ways.

... I do not mean literally have Christ in our thoughts every moment, but rather ... have faith in Him at the bottom of our thoughts, as the foundation upon which they all rest."

Hannah Whitall Smith (adapted)

The books you read may have much to
do with your choosing of the road.
Katherine Logan

"Keeping mentally fit has to do with your mind — thinking straight, clear and clean ... To keep mentally fit for right living one must refuse wrong thoughts ...

There is a positive approach to this problem which has helped many. Refuse to have a negative, listless attitude ... Where the mind is given to healthful, positive thinking, little place is left for the entrance of unwanted, debasing thoughts. Memorizing Scripture gives valuable assistance ... Such good things return to one's mind in unoccupied moments, the very times undesirable suggestions seek to intrude.

Consider the wealth of good books today ... If a mind feeds on the soul-destroying literature which floods the bookstands today, evil thoughts and suggestions will follow automatically. *'Tell me what you eat and I'll tell you what you are'* was the slogan many years ago for a certain breakfast food. It is the unquestionable truth in the realm of the mind as well —"

Alice Reynolds Flower (adapted)

Hugs and Listening

"Gentle ... like a mother who cares for her children" (1 Thessalonians 2:7).

"You do know that hearing and listening aren't the same? When we were on a trip, we ended up in an ice-cream parlor, and there were so many flavors available. My husband makes dozens of business decisions a day, and he was quick. He said, 'I'll have pistachio.' 'Is that the green kind?' I asked. But he was signaling to the waitress, and I said again, 'Is that the green kind?' By this time the waitress had arrived and he said, 'Two pistachios, please.'

It came, and it was green. And I wailed, 'That's why I asked you! I don't like the green kind.' At that moment the Holy Spirit spoke to me so clearly, *'That's exactly how your kids feel when they come to pour out their hearts to you, and you keep right on doing what you were doing, and say, "Mm-hm." They know you're not really listening, and eventually they will quit trying.'*

Later when you *want* your children to talk to you, they may close the door. Don't just hear your children, *look* at them and really *listen!*"

June Hurst

"One summer evening when I was twelve I was helping my mother take down the clothes. We had a clothesline strung from the large hickory tree in our backyard to the two oak trees ... We worked in harmony as we took down a large white sheet, folded it together, and laid it in the clothes basket. Then, instead of taking down the next sheet, she stopped, put her arms around me, and gave me a hug. I was taken by surprise, but I remember that it felt good. Often in the years to come, when we were separated by continents, I was warmed by the memory of that unexpected hug."

Ingrid Trobisch

"The spirit of affection ... let no one shrink from expressing it! The heart has strange abysses of gloom, and often yearns for just one word of love to help. And it is just when the manner may be less genial than usual that the need may be greatest."

Lucy C. Smith (adapted)

"We all need encouragement. We can live without it just as a young tree can live without fertilizer, but unless we receive that warm nurturing, we never reach our full potential, and like the tree left to itself, we seldom bear fruit."

Florence Littauer

"A family ... is a group of people who, when you hurt, show that they care ... *'Home is the place where, when you have to go there, they have to take you in.'* ... These words from the beloved poet Robert Frost have sparked in me an amused and understanding attitude — as I have watched the family come home, one by one — happy or sad, angry or 'hyper,' fighting or withdrawn. ... But because we are a 'colony of caring,' we open the door, hold out our arms and love!"

Arvella Schuller

Expectations

"Am I now seeking the favo of people or of God? Am I trying to ple^se people? I am not a servant of Chris⸱ i,' I am still trying to please people" (Galatians 1:10).

"Sometimes the Lord can be pushed into the background by our consciousness of the opinions of people, what they think we ought to be and do.

When we first became pastors, I tried so hard to be what people expected that I lost perspective. Once the church was having special meetings. I had taken our children to the services every night for several weeks. Finally our little six-year-old daughter was becoming very nervous and jumpy. My heart told me the children needed a night at home, but I was torn between being a good example to the people and doing what I felt I should as a mother.

My husband found me in tears and asked what was wrong. When I told him, he said, 'Honey, what do you think the Lord wants you to do?' 'Well,' I said, 'I really feel He wants me to stay home and put the kids in bed, read them a story and pray with them, and let them sleep tonight.' He said, 'Then do it.' And I said, 'What will the people think?'

My husband said something that really changed things for me. He said, *'If you please God, you will please the people He wants you to please.'*

I experienced a great release that day when I realized that if I do my best to please God, I can leave the rest to Him ... What *'they'* think can put a heavy load on us, but when we are thinking about what *He* thinks, there is joy in trying to please Him."

Oriole Dover

"You must remember that our God has all knowledge and all wisdom, and that therefore it is very possible He may guide you into paths where He knows great blessings are awaiting you, but which to the short-sighted human eyes around you seem sure to result in confusion and loss ... He alone, who knows the end of things from the beginning, can judge what the results of any course of action may be. You must therefore realize that His very love for you may lead you to run counter to the loving wishes of even your dearest friends.

... The child of God who enters on this life of obedience ... can trust the Lord through it all."

Hannah Whitall Smith (adapted)

Cheerfulness

"A cheerful look brings joy to the heart"
(Proverbs 15:30 niv).

"It seems as if God gathered into His storehouse, from each of our lives, fruit in which He delights ... the bright word spoken when head and heart are weary ... the steady going on in one unbroken round, with a patient cheerfulness that knows nothing of 'moods' — all these are gathered there and add to our riches toward Him."

Hetty Bowman (adapted)

Give me, O Lord, a heart of grace,
A voice of joy, a shining face,
That I may show where'er I turn
Thy love within my soul doth burn!
A tenderness for all that stray,
With strength to help them on the way.
A cheerfulness, a heavenly mirth,
Brightening my steps along the earth.
Lady Gilbert

"If you have a murmuring spirit, you cannot have true cheerfulness — it will generally show in your countenance and your voice. Some little fretfulness or restlessness of tone will betray it."

Priscilla Maurice

God give me sympathy and sense
And help me keep my courage high;
God give me calm and confidence,
And — please — a twinkle in my eye.

Margaret Bailey

"Then saw I that each kind compassion that man hath on his fellow-Christians with charity, it is Christ in him."

Mother Juliana

"Happiness ... is as truly our portion here as above. It cannot fail to fall within the lot of those who have chosen for their portion Him whose nature is Joy. God, in communicating himself to the soul, of necessity communicates happiness, and all souls in union with Him are happy, in exact proportion to the closeness and fullness of their union — happy, in other words, by so much as they have within them of God."

Dora Greenwell (adapted)

It takes so little to make us sad,
Just a slighting word or a
doubting sneer,
Just a scornful smile on some lips
held dear,
And our footsteps lag, though the goal
seemed near.
And we lose the courage and hope
we had,
So little it takes to make us sad.

It takes so little to make us glad,
Just a cheering clasp of a friendly hand,
Just a word from one who
can understand,
And we finish the task we long
had planned.
And we lose the doubt and fear we had,
So little it takes to make us glad.

Author Unknown

"Thank God for the smilers
in the world."

Where We Look

"My eyes are ever toward the Lord, for He will pluck my feet out of the net" (Psalm 25:15).

"It is a fact that we see what we look at ... and we cannot look unto Jesus while we are looking at ourselves. The power for victory and endurance are to come from looking unto Jesus and considering Him, not from looking unto or considering ourselves, or our circumstances, or our sins, or our temptations. Looking at ourselves causes weakness and defeat. ... The remedy and the supply are not in self but in Christ. ... But self is always determined to secure attention, and would rather be thought badly of than not to be thought of at all.

... I was very much helped many years ago by the following sentence by Adelaide Procter: *'For one look at self take ten looks at Christ.'* It was entirely contrary to all I had previously thought right, but it carried conviction to my soul, and delivered me from a habit of morbid self-examination and introspection that had made my life miserable for years. It was an unspeakable deliverance ...

(God) calls upon us to forget our selves and to go to work to lessen the miseries of others ... to give up our efforts to find something in ourselves to delight in, and delight ourselves only in the Lord.

... The only road to Christlikeness is to behold His goodness and beauty. We grow like what we look at ... We must say with the psalmist: *'I have set the Lord* [not self] *always before me; because He is at my right hand, I shall not be moved. Therefore my heart is glad.'"*

Hannah Whitall Smith (adapted)

"Your feelings will ebb and flow ... you will be brave and steadfast today, downcast and anxious tomorrow ... Turn away from yourself! Hope in God! He faints not, nor is He weary ... with Him is no variableness, neither shadow of turning. When you are dismayed, He is still eternal peace."

Selected (adapted)

Our Gifts

"But all these gifts are the work of the same Spirit, who gives them to each person, as He chooses" (1 Corinthians 12:11).

"Gifts are given *'to every man according to his several ability.'* That is, we have just as much given as God knows we are able to use and what we can best use for Him. *'But unto every one of us is given grace according to the measure of the gift of Christ.'*

[By] claiming and using that grace, you can do more for God than the mightiest intellect in the world without it.

... The Holy Spirit is just as able to draw a soul to Jesus, if He will, by your whisper of the one word, "Come," as by an eloquent sermon an hour long.

He who made every power can use every power — memory, judgment, imagination ... musical, poetical, oratorical, or artistic faculty; special tastes for reasoning, philosophy, history, natural science, or natural history — all these may be dedicated to Him, sanctified by Him, and used by Him.

Whatever He has given, He will use if we will let Him. Often in the most unexpected ways ... something read or acquired long ago suddenly comes into use. We cannot foresee what will thus 'come in useful,' but He knew, when He guided us to learn it, what it would be wanted for in His service. So may we not ask Him to guide us to what He knows there will be use for in the work to which He has called us?

... The Lord makes the most of whatever is unreservedly surrendered to Him ... He wastes no material."

Frances Ridley Havergal (adapted)

God's gifts put
man's best dreams to shame.
Elizabeth Barrett Browning

"Success is living in such a way that you are using what God has given you — your intellect, abilities and energy — to reach the purpose that He intends for your life."
Kathi Hudson

Be Still

"The Lord will fight for you, and you have only to be still" (Exodus 14:14 rsv).

"I have not found that illness makes prayer easier, nor do any of our family who have been ill tell me that they have found it so ... A bed can be a place of dullness of spirit as well as of body, and prayer is, after all, work.

... One night, soon after neuritis had taken possession of me from shoulder blade to fingertips, I could no more gather myself up to pray than I could turn in bed without help ... But I could read, and I opened on Psalm 109: *'Do Thou for me, O God the Lord.'* Do what? It does not say. It just says, 'Do Thou for me.'

And the prayer, so simple, so easy for a tired heart, had a delivering power. ... And soon the prayer passed into the most restful kind of intercession, the only kind the ill can attain unto, for they cannot pray in detail and they may know little or nothing of the needs of their dearest.

But He knows all, down to the smallest wish of the heart. So we do not need to coin our gold in words, we could not if we tried: we are far too tired for that; and He who knows our frame does not ask us to do anything so arduous: *'Do Thou for her, do Thou for him, do Thou for them, O God the Lord.'* This word of peace greatly eased my spirit ..."

Amy Carmichael (adapted)

Be still, my soul —
for just as thou art still,
Can God reveal Himself to thee, until
Through thee His love and light and life
can freely flow.
In stillness God can work through thee
and reach
The souls around thee. He then through
thee can teach
His lessons — and His power in
weakness show.

Bessie Porter

"Meditate in your heart upon your bed, and be still" (Psalm 4:4 nasb).

Inasmuch

"Complete this work by doing what you are able to do" (2 Corinthians 8:11)

"We first went to Tanganyika as the only missionaries of our denomination in the country. The Christians were eager for a Bible school. By the Lord's help, in seven months we built the buildings, and my husband and I both taught from morning to night. We were so thrilled and busy we didn't have time to be lonely.

As time went on, new missionaries joined us; missionaries from other denominations found us; we met colonial settlers ... they all seemed drawn to our home. The next few years every time my husband was ready to go do mission work, I'd hear that a family or two were coming to stay with us.

So it was up to me to stay home, keep our house ready, and entertain the guests. I realized each of these families *needed* to come, not only for food and supplies, but for fellowship and encouragement. But I felt resentment building up. One year from January to October I changed over 290 guest beds and cooked hundreds of meals. Then one day — I'll never forget it — I was in the guest rooms, pulling off still-warm sheets to put on fresh ones before somebody else arrived. I felt so miserable, and dissatisfied, and I said, 'God, I came here to bring your Word, and work with my husband. All I'm doing is entertaining, running a hotel.' And then He whispered in my heart, '*Inasmuch as ye have done it unto one of the least of these My brethren, ye have done it unto Me.*'

I cried, 'O God, forgive me.' I realized that this was the ministry He had placed in my hands and I wasn't even aware of it. I said, 'Lord, every time I change a sheet from now on, I'm going to change it with You, and every meal I cook I'm going to prepare it for You.' I did that, and I found a new joy welling up that I had never experienced before.

... I believe our goal should be not to have preconceived ideas of what we will do, but whatever our hands find to do, do it with all of our hearts. This is all He asks us to do. Just live one day at a time ... Walk through the doors He opens ... And accept that which He offers us to do. If we do it in a spirit of love and commitment, He says *'even a cup of cold water will not go without its reward.'*"

June Hurst

... The quickened heart to know
God's will
And on His errands run.

Susan Coolidge

"Take each thing as it comes to you, and look upon it as the present expression of the will of God concerning you; then regard the next in the same way, and thus receive your day piece by piece from Him who will remember always when He gives you work to do, that you need strength to do it."

Priscilla Maurice

"Another step, so simple that it is often despised, is to do everything, however ordinary, as well as it can possibly be done, for God's sake."

Henrietta Louisa Sidney Lear

The Snarls of Life

"God's power guards you through faith ... even though you have suffered greatly in all kinds of troubles for a short time now" (1 Peter 1:5,6).

"I have always been glad that the Psalmist said to God that some things were hard. There is no mistake about it — there are hard things in life. Some beautiful pink flowers were given me this summer, and as I took them I said, 'What are they?' And the answer came, 'They are rock flowers. They grow and bloom only on rocks where you can see no soil.' Then I thought of God's flowers growing in hard places, and I feel somehow that He may have a peculiar tenderness for His 'rock flowers' that He may not have for His lilies and roses."

Margaret Bottome

"No matter what sort of a snarl I may have been in, whether inward or outward,

I have always found that while I kept my eyes on the snarl and tried to unravel it, it grew worse and worse; but when I turned my eyes away from the snarl and kept them fixed on the Lord, He always sooner or later delivered me."

Hannah Whitall Smith

When obstacles and trials seem
Like prison walls to be,
I do the little I can do,
And leave the rest to Thee.
F. W. F.

"When life caves in, we are to seek God in our problem. God has a plan for every life by which He will bring good out of evil."

Catherine Marshall

"When we stand in the middle of a lifestorm, it seems as if the storm has become our way of life. We cannot see a way out. ... We feel defeated — and broken. Will that brokenness ... keep us forever in the mire of 'if only' thinking? Or will we yield up that brokenness to the resources of the One who calms the winds and the waves, heals the brokenhearted,

and forgives the most grievous of sins?
The choice is ours."

Verdell Davis

To Thee I bring my care,
The care I cannot flee.
Thou wilt not only share,
But bear it all for me.
O loving Saviour, now to Thee,
I bring the load that wearies me.

Frances R. Havergal

"The Shepherd said ... 'Remember, even though you seem to be farther away than ever ... from Me, there is really no distance at all separating us. I can cross the desert sands as swiftly as I can leap from the High Places to the valleys, and whenever you call for me, I shall come.'"

Hannah Hurnard

Not Just Icing

"I continually remember you in my prayers night and day" (1 Timothy 1:3).

"Perhaps we do not think enough what an effective service prayer is, especially intercessory prayer. We do not believe as we should how it might help those we so long to serve, penetrating the hearts we cannot open, shielding those we cannot guard, teaching where we cannot speak, comforting where our words have no power to soothe, following the steps of those we love through the toils and perplexities of the day, lifting off their burdens with an unseen hand at night. No ministry is so like that of an angel as this — silent, invisible, known only to God."

Elizabeth Rundle Charles (adapted)

"God has given us prayer to have a realistic 'work' that can be done in prison, in a wheel chair, in bed in a hospital or a hovel or a palace, on the march, in the midst of battle ... Prayer is not just icing on the cake of a so-called spiritual life; prayer is warm, close communication with the living God, and also a matter of doing an active work on His side of the battle."

Edith Schaeffer

There's no weapon half so mighty
As the intercessors bear,
Nor a broader field of service
Than the ministry of prayer.
Author Unknown

"I cannot tell why there should come to me a thought of someone miles and years away, in swift insistence on the memory, unless there is a need that I should pray."

Rosalind Goforth, missionary to China

In prayer we gain
an invisible force
which will triumph over
seemingly hopeless difficulties.
H. L. Sidney Lear

"I cannot stress too much the untapped power and inner strength to change persons, homes and churches, because we too often take for granted and neglect this glorious access to God, and this ministry to those we love, and to our own growth."

Sara Abram

"It's been said that faith may move mountains, but prayer moves God. Amazing, isn't it, that our prayers, whether grand and glorious or feeble and faint, can move the very heart of God who created the universe?"

Joni Eareckson Tada

Self-Defense

"Dearly beloved, avenge not yourselves"
(Romans 12:19).

"There are seasons when to be *still* demands immeasurably higher strength than to act.

... To the most deadly charges Jesus responded with deep, unbroken silence ... Those who are unjustly accused and causelessly ill-treated know what tremendous strength is necessary to keep silence to God.

> Men may misjudge thy aim,
> Think they have cause to blame,
> Say thou art wrong;
> Keep on thy quiet way,
> Christ is the Judge, not they,
> Fear not, be strong.

St. Paul said, *'None of these things move me.'* He did not say, *'None of these things hurt me.'* It is one thing to be hurt and quite another to be moved. ... The apostle had determined not to move from what he believed was right ... he did not care for ease ... he cared for only one thing, and that was to be loyal to Christ, to have His smile."

Margaret Bottome (adapted)

"The Roman soldiers were surrounding his Master, and Peter rose at once in defense ... But from our Savior's lips came ... *'Put up thy sword into the sheath: the cup which My Father hath given Me shall I not drink it?'* ... To Peter came this added word of mild reproof, *'All they that take the sword shall perish with the sword.'*

We are frequently tempted to 'take the sword' in our own defense. A false accusation has been made ... every ounce of self-preservation urges us to strike back. But our attempts at self-vindication are seldom successful. So often the more we struggle to clear ourselves, the more complicated the matter becomes. Then in desperation we cry, *'Lord, You avenge me of my adversary and straighten out this mess.'* Not until then do we have peace and victory.

Sometimes disagreeing parties can meet face to face and come to a fair understanding. ... But the situation is not always so simply adjusted ... Your desire is right, yet your best efforts for peace are being misjudged. What can you do?

'Rest in the Lord and wait patiently for him' to work it out. ... If you can keep your hand off that sword, and leave your reputation, your fears, your heart wounds — everything — in His loving hands, you will be amazed at what God will do in your behalf.

... This also applies when we want to defend those we love, as did Peter. God wants us to be loyal ... but ... when your words of defense become swords of fighting, you have gone too far. Simply *'put up your sword'* and leave the cause to the ... God (who) may be working in all concerned a new measure of love and grace.

Alice Reynolds Flower (adapted)

"A moment's silence, when some irritating words are said may seem a very small thing; yet at that moment it is your one duty, your one way of serving and pleasing God, and if you break it, you have lost your opportunity."

Henrietta Louisa Sidney Lear (adapted)

It's the Same As

"Hath He said, and will He not do it? Or hath He spoken, and will He not make it good?" (Numbers 23:19)

"When my little son was about ten years of age, his grandmother promised him a stamp album for Christmas.

Christmas came, but no stamp album, and no word from grandmother ... but when his playmates came to see his Christmas present, I was astonished, after he had named over this and that as gifts received, to hear him add, 'And a stamp album from Grandmother.'

I called him to me, and said, 'But Georgie, you did not get an album from your grandmother. Why do you say so?'

There was a wondering look on his face, as if he thought it strange that I should ask such a question, and he replied, 'Well, Mama, Grandma *said*, so it's the same as.'

... A month went by, and nothing was

heard from the album. Finally one day I said ... 'Well, Georgie, I think Grandma has forgotten her promise.'

"Oh, no, Mama,' he quickly and firmly said, 'she hasn't.'

I watched the trusting face, which for awhile looked very sober, as if debating the possibilities I had suggested. Finally a bright light passed over it, and he said, 'Mama, do you think it would do any good if I should write to her thanking her for the album?'

... A rich spiritual truth began to dawn upon me. In a few minutes a letter was mailed and he went off whistling his confidence in his grandma. In just a short time a letter came, saying:

My dear Georgie,

I have not forgotten my promise to you of an album. I tried to get such a book as you desired, but could not get the sort you wanted, so I sent on to New York. It did not get here till after Christmas, and it was still not right, so I sent for another, and as it has not come as yet, I send you money to get one in Chicago.

Your loving Grandma.

As he read the letter, his face was the face of a victor. 'Now, Mama, didn't I tell you?' came from a heart that never doubted, that *against hope, believed in hope* that the stamp album would come. While he was trusting, Grandma was working, and in due season faith became sight.

It is so human to want sight when we step out on the promises of God, but our Saviour said to Thomas, and to the long line of doubters who have ever since followed him, *'Blessed are they who have not seen, and yet have believed.'*

Mrs. Rounds (adapted)

Dear restless heart, be still;
Don't fret and worry so;
God has a thousand ways
His love and help to show;
Just trust, and trust, and trust,
Until His will you know.

Edith Willis Linn

"You who are evil know how to give good gifts to your children, so won't your Father who is in heaven want even more to give good things to the people who ask Him?" (Matthew 7:11)

This Thing is From Me

"This thing is from Me" *(1 Kings 12:24).*

"My child, I have a message for you today. Let me whisper it in your ear, that it may smooth the rough places upon which you may have to tread. It is short, only five words, but let them sink into your inmost soul. Use them as a pillow upon which to rest your weary head. *This thing is from me.*

I would have you learn when temptations assail you, and the 'enemy comes in like a flood,' that *this thing is from Me*, that your weakness needs My might, and your safety lies in letting Me fight for you.

Are you in difficult circumstances, surrounded by people who do not understand you? *This thing is from Me.* I am the God of circumstances. You did not come to this place by accident, it is the very place God meant for you.

Are you in money difficulties? Is it hard to make both ends meet? *This thing is from Me*, for I would have you draw from and depend upon Me. My supplies are limitless.

'My God will give you everything you need, by His ... riches through Jesus Christ' (Philippians 4:19).

I would have you prove My promises.

Are you passing through a night of sorrow? *This thing is from Me*. I am the Man of Sorrows and acquainted with grief. I have let earthly comforters fail you, that by turning to Me you may obtain everlasting consolation.

'May our Lord Jesus Christ, and God our Father who loved us and gave us everlasting comfort ... encourage you and make you strong' (2 Thessalonians 2:16,17).

Have you longed to do some great work for Me and instead have been laid aside on a bed of pain and weakness? *This thing is from Me* ... I want to teach you some of my deepest lessons. ... Some of My greatest workers are those shut out from active service, that they may learn to wield the weapon of all-prayer.

This day I place in your hand this holy oil ... Let every circumstance that arises, every word that pains you, every interruption that would make you impatient, every revelation of your weakness be anointed with it. The sting will go as you learn to *see Me in all things*."

Laura A. Barter Snow (adapted)

I thank Thee, O God,
for the relief and satisfaction of mind
that come with the firm assurance
that Thou dost govern the world ...
that even the tumultuous and irregular
actions of sinful men
are, nevertheless, under Thy direction,
who ... hast promised to make
all things
work together for good
to them that love Thee.

Susanna Wesley

"This way of seeing our Father in everything makes life one long thanksgiving and gives a rest of heart, and, more than that, a gayety of spirit, that is unspeakable."

Hannah Whitall Smith

The Waves of Doubt

"But have faith when you ask, and do not doubt. The person who doubts is like the waves of the sea that the wind blows up and down" (James 1:6).

"The whole root and cause then of our wavering experience is not, as we may have thought, our sins, but is simply and only our doubts. Doubts create an impassable gulf between our souls and the Lord, just as inevitably as they do between us and our earthly friends

... This is not because God is angry and visits His displeasure on the man who doubts, but it is because of that inherent nature of things that makes it impossible for doubt and confidence to exist together.

... Faith is the only door into the kingdom of heaven ... If we will not go in by that door, we cannot get in at all, for there is no other way.

The one question is how to put an end at once and forever to wavering. I am thankful to say I know of a perfect remedy ... Your wavering is caused by your doubting ... Give up your doubting, and your wavering will stop.

... Perhaps it has never entered your head that you could give up doubting altogether. But I assert that you can. You can simply refuse to doubt. You can shut the door against every suggestion of doubt that comes, and can by faith declare exactly the opposite. Your doubt says, *'God does not forgive my sins.'* Your faith must say, *'He does forgive me, He says He does, and I choose to believe Him. I am His forgiven child.'* And you must assert this steadfastly, until all your doubts vanish.

... Let nothing shake your faith. Should even sin unhappily overtake you, you must not let it make you doubt ... this is only to add a new sin to the one already committed.

Return at once to God in the way the Bible teaches, and let your faith hold steadfastly to His Word. Believe it, not because you feel it, or see it, but because He says it.

... Believe it actively and steadfastly, through dark and through light, through ups and through downs, through times of comfort and through times of despair, and I can promise you, without a fear, that your wavering experience will be ended."

Hannah Whitall Smith (adapted)

"I know one can go on doing one's duty under clouds of doubt ... There are many who do, and they are dear to God, but the duty is done sadly, without the spring of life and joy that we are meant to have. That fountain of life and strength is hid in God. Christ showed us the way to it, and we get it into our souls when we utterly trust Him."

Annie Keary (adapted)

The Way, the Truth, the Life Thou art,
This, this I know — to this I cleave,
The sweet new language of my heart
'Lord, I believe.'
I have no doubts to bring to Thee,
My doubt has fled, my faith is free.
Harriet McEwen Kimball

In His Quietness

"Study to be quiet" (1 Thessalonians 4:11).

"'*In quietness and in confidence shall be your strength,*' we are told by the Word of God. Where men of the world might rush about frantic and disturbed, the child of God, walking in His will, can well afford to step quietly aside and watch to see God work. He has proved what it is to *'Stand still and see the salvation of the Lord.'*

A quiet spirit speaks of confidence and of humility, seeing our resources not in ourselves, but in the Lord. Of this attitude, Andrew Murray says: 'Humility is perfect quietness of heart ... It is to have a blessed home in the Lord, where I can go in and shut the door, and kneel to my Father in secret, at peace as in a deep sea of calmness, when all around and above is trouble.'

Has not Christ made all that relates to us His own intimate concern? Is He not our shepherd? Has He not taken the responsibility of His sheep?

... Job, in the midst of his bewildering losses of children, cattle, and riches, learned to say, *'He giveth quietness.'* It is in our difficult hours that we too can learn that quietness is not from our circumstances but from God himself.

... Artists were once trying for a prize for painting the best picture of 'Peace.' Some chose lovely sunsets, some quiet meadows: but the one who won the prize painted a terrific storm in the woods, lightning crashing, torrents of rain falling. High on an over-covered bough swung a sheltered nest. In it, snug and contented, nestled the little birds in perfect confidence. They were quiet and at peace amid the storm. Such is God's loving watch-care to us that we, too, can be as contented as they, and amid sunshine or storm as satisfied and as quiet."

Zelma Argue

"By Thy grace may my mind ... be kept calm and composed ... I have found that the still, small voice is not heard amidst the thunder and noise of tumultuous passions. Keep then, my mind ... Be pleased, often in the day, to call it in from outward objects, lest it wander ..."

The Prayers of Susanna Wesley (adapted)

From the world of sin, and noise,
And hurry, I withdraw;
For the small and inward voice
I wait with humble awe;
Silent am I now, and still ...
To my waiting soul reveal
The secret of Thy love.

Hymn

"I do not believe that we have begun to understand the marvelous power there is in stillness. We are in such a hurry — we must be doing — so that we are in danger of not giving God a chance to work. You may depend on it, God never says to us, *'Stand still,'* or *'Sit still,'* or *'Be still,'* unless He is going to do something."

(Selected)

"How rare it is to find a soul quiet enough to hear God speak."

A Radiating Love

"Love is from God. ... No one has seen God at any time, but God lives in us, and His love is made complete in us if we love each other" (1 John 4:7,12).

"He has created us to love. We have a sealed treasure of love which either remains sealed and then gradually dries up ... or is unsealed and poured out ... the fuller and not the emptier for the outpouring. The more love we give, the more we have to give. So far it is only natural. But when the Holy Spirit sheds abroad the love of God in our hearts, this natural love is penetrated with a new principle.

... The love of Christ is not an absorbing but a radiating love. The more we love Him, the more we shall most certainly love others. Some have not much natural power of loving, but the love of Christ will strengthen it. Some have had the springs of love dried up by some terrible earthquake.

They will find fresh springs in Jesus, and the gentle flow will be purer and deeper than the old torrent could ever be. Some have been satisfied that it should rush in a narrow channel, but He will cause it to overflow ... and widen its course of blessing. Some have spent it all on their God-given dear ones. ... He puts back an even larger measure of the old love into our hand, sanctified with His own love and energized with His new command, *'That ye love one another, as I have loved you.'* In drawing others to ourselves ... we shall be necessarily drawing them nearer to the Fountain of our love."

Frances Ridley Havergal (adapted)

"As each sister is to become a co-worker of Christ ... let Christ radiate and live His life in her and through her ... let the poor, seeing her, be drawn to Christ and invite Him to enter their homes and their lives. Let the sick and suffering find in her a real angel of comfort and consolation. Let the little ones of the streets cling to her because she reminds them of Him, the friend of the little ones."

Mother Teresa